SN

# PRAISE FOR HOTHEAD PAISAN

"When I present my work in bookstores across the country, I always ask lesbian audiences what they most love to read. The answer is unanimous: *Hothead Paisan*. It's the bible of man-hating ball busters driven over the edge of insanity into our own state where anarchy reigns and no man is safe to walk the streets. A blueprint for mind-expanding universal retribution and revenge." —**Sarah Schulman**

"*Hothead Paisan* is an irresistible fusion of violence, television, caffeine, sex and spiritual enlightenment. DON'T READ Hothead and Chicken and their stunning arsenal of wit unless you're prepared for explosive thought and violent laughter." —**Jenny Livingston**, writer/director, *Paris Is Burning*

"Finally, an escape from the suffocating craziness of the everyday. Hothead Paisan, the Homicidal Lesbian Terrorist, answers the question *Is it them or is it me?* in a radically feminist, murderously funny way. Definitely a book for public transportation—any annoying someone with half a brain would move ten feet away from a person reading this..." —**Jacqueline Woodson**

"Hothead's got fans out there lined up like metal shavings before a magnet..." —**Kris Kovick**

"Ever had some idiot yell something about your tits and wish you had an AK-47 hiding right there under your jacket? Of course, most of us are never going to take the extremist route to female liberation, but we can dream...Hothead Paisan helps us right down the path. Hothead is a raging city dyke with scary hair and a fetish for guns, grenades, mallets and sharp objects." —*Brat Attack*

"Hothead Paisan [is] an unabashedly lesbocentric, literally male-bashing, spiritually enlightening and wildly funny comic, with the weaponry to make the difference." —*The Women's Review of Books*

"Hothead is the biggest stroke of genius in queer cartooning yet...watching Hothead unleash her rage is great revenge on a fucked up world...Hey, it's a lot cheaper than therapy, and it'll make ya laugh, too." —**Rachel Pepper**, *Bay Area Reporter*

"Hothead attracts a fanatical following that crosses lines of gender and orientation. Hothead is an equal opportunity avenger...Hothead practices preventative homicide." —*Frighten the Horses*

"I think it would do America a lot of good if everybody tested her or his tolerance levels for whatever each of us finds intolerable, and almost everyone can find something worth testing in *Hothead Paisan: Homicidal Lesbian Terrorist*." —*Spectator*

Diane DiMassa's "cartooning style is electric." —**Howard Cruse**

"Yow! Hothead makes Bitchy Bitch look like a wimp." —**Roberta Gregory**

"Definitely outrageous and a lot of fun. These women have attitude." —*The World of Zines*

# HOTHEAD PAISAN

# HOTHEAD PAISAN

## HOMICIDAL LESBIAN TERRORIST

### DIANE DIMASSA

CLEIS
PRESS

Published in the United States by Cleis Press Inc., P.O. Box 8933, Pittsburgh, Pennsylvania 15221, and P.O. Box 14684, San Francisco, California 94114.

Book production: Pete Ivey
Cleis logo art: Juana Alicia

Printed in the United States of America
10 9 8 7 6 5 4 3 2 1


*Library of Congress Cataloging-in-Publication Data*

DiMassa, Diane, 1959–
    Hothead Paisan : homicidal lesbian terrorist / by Diane DiMassa.
        p.  cm.
    ISBN: 0-939416-73-5 : $12.95
    I. Title.
PN6727.D56H67   1993                              93-6259
741.5'973—dc20                                    CIP

This book is dedicated
to all the women who are not afraid,
and to all the women who are.

We are grateful to The All That Is, Karen Aiken, S. Bryn Austin, Jamie
Bargas, Alison Bechdel, Nancy Boutilier, Doug Brantley, Elaine Brown,
Marleen Cenotti, Sue Czark, Frédérique Delacoste, Laura Ernst Downey
and Robert Downey, Fish, Lisa Frank, Eleanor Craig Green, Anne
Griepenburg, Ann Grossman, Kris Kovick, The Lesbian Avengers, Jennie
Livingston, Eileen McGuigan, Mom's one and only turkey, Felice Newman,
Beryl Normand, Heather Pearl, Rachel Pepper, Sarah Pettit, Roxxie, Deb
Schwartz, Carol Seajay, John Searles, Lauren Seeley, Iggy Sheehan and
Frank Sheehan, Gail Simon, Victoria Starr, Franco Stevens, Roz Warren,
Alice Winn, Jody Wheat, David Wilk and Steve Hargraves and the
cowpokes of Dead Rat Head Canyon (Sheriff Owen, Deirdre, Jeanne, Suzy,
Doug, Nancy, Dennis, Jay, Dave, Gary and Jared), who saw it all begin.

And, of course, to our families, whose support has never been taken for
less than the grand thing that it is.

To all the people who threw Hothead Paisan in the garbage, then took it
back out, then threw it back in, then ripped it up, then asked us for
another copy...

To all our sister 'zinesters: keep it up, grrrls!

To all the women's studies, lesbian and gay studies, and cultural studies
teachers who have seen a light in this work and have shared it, we bow,
smile, and thank you.

To the nameless friends who found delight in Hothead Paisan and passed
us on to friends, we bow and kiss your toes.

And, finally, to the great goddesses and gods of the feline purrsuasion:
without you we are bored, unloved, and unable to exist.

# Introduction

Hothead Paisan is angry. Maybe she wouldn't be quite so furious if everybody took up equal amounts of space in the world. Hothead is a flaming mouthpiece for those who must remember to remember day after day that they are not less worthy, less deserving, less anything. Sadly, some people never come to believe this about themselves. This is most definitely planned: it is a set-up intended to keep people disempowered.

Hothead Paisan is, among other things, a battler for the right to take up a little space. She's a blend of childlike bewilderment—how could things have gotten so rotten?—and unapologetic reaction to the monsters around her. Autobiographical? Of course she is. Hothead Paisan was born in my journal, a personal vent, the result of my desperate search for a way to purge my own rage without getting injured. The disturbing images that I draw are just that—disturbing. These images are in my gut; it would be a disaster to pretend they're not. Anger sits like poison when ignored and grows into mutant proportions. None of us can afford that. By getting these images out into the light, where they can be examined, I can then move on.

So what began as my personal medicine has made its way into the world, thanks to Stacy Sheehan, who publishes *Hothead Paisan* four times a year in comic-zine form under the Giant Ass imprint. It was because of Stacy's urging and innate rainmaking sense that *Hothead Paisan* was developed, printed, distributed. She is the mechanic behind the workings, and is the reason that *Hothead Paisan*, the comic-zine, originally appeared in your store, your home, your hands. And the response has been...more than we ever dreamed. We receive letters from people of all descriptions (and I do mean ALL) who fight each day not to get backed into that little corner where they feel like they are insane, or completely alone, or freaks...They are family, and we're proud to be among them.

People ask me if Hothead will ever calm down. I feel that she only reflects what is going on "out there," so I don't see her changing very soon. The magic is that Hothead's behavior allows ME to be a calmer person. I hope for the day when she *can* calm down! But for now, Hothead will continue to act out the fantasies that we would never really carry out ourselves, even though we're thinking them.

Considering the constant onslaught of hostility and hate and frightening levels of intolerance we are subject to every day, if Hothead serves to remind you that you are wonderful and not alone, then what more can this Paisan ask? May the spirit of Hothead always walk with you and slay all your dragons.

Love and peace,

*Diane DiMassa*

*August 1993*

9

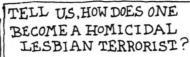

WHO CAN RESIST THE FASCINATION OF MONSTER TRUKS OR WRESTLING??

OR FIVE WHITE GUYS IN SUITS DECIDING THE FATE OF THE WORLD AS A RESULT OF THE CATASTRO-PHIES THEY CAUSED??

OR FOR THOSE REALLY BRAIN-DEAD DAYS, YOU CAN **ALWAYS** FIND A MACHO CAR CHASE OR SOME HELPLESS **BROAD** BEING RESCUED!

BECAUSE SHE JUST **TRIPPED**, OF COURSE!

AND MY PERSONAL FAV'RIT: AN ENTIRE SERIES ABOUT THE FIRST HORMONAL STIRRINGS OF A PRE-PUBESCENT YOU-KNOW-WHAT!!

GOD, THIS IS **GREAT!!**

AND DONT LETS FORGET THE FAMILY SITCOMS, WHERE THE BOYS FIX THE CARS AND THE GIRLS BAKE CAKES AND THE BOYS LAUGH AT THE GIRLS CAUSE THE GIRLS ARE JUST SILLY CAUSE THE MOTHER IS A MOM-BOT AND FATHER IS A DICK AND IT RUNS IN THE FAMILY.

OH YEH, AND THE **NEWS**, THE BIGGEST HORROR SHOW OF 'EM ALL.

SIR, DID YOU IN FACT SHOOT YOUR WIFE?

HOW THE FUCK SHOULD AH KNOW? AH WAZ DRUNKER 'N HELL! AH THANK OUR DAUGHTER DID IT.

POOR MAN!

15

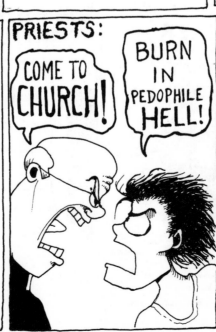

20

I WONDER WHAT WOULD HAPPEN IF SAY, SOME LESBIAN REALLY CHECKED OUT FOR LUNCH, YOU KNOW, LIKE SAY HER BRAIN JUST TOTALLY SHIT THE BED ONE DAY, AND SHE STARTS BELIEVING EVERYTHING SHE SEES ON T.V. SO LIKE, WHILE SHE'S GOING ABOUT HER DAILY QUEER ROUTINE, ALL THIS T.V. CRAP IS SEEPING IN AND SHE'S GETTING PSYCHOTIC, AND LIKE SHE NEEDS THERAPY REALLY BAD, BUT SHE DOESN'T KNOW IT? I BET HER BOUNDARIES WOULD BE REALLY FUZZY. I BET SHE'D BE LOTS OF FUN TO BE AROUND. I BET SHE'D BE A REAL...

# HOTHEAD PAISAN

by mommy St. wee-wee    ©1991

IS IT A MAGIC MICROPHONE?
♪ I LEFT MY DICK... IN SAN FRANCISCO ♪
HEY! wake up mr. right one, yer missin the show!

IS IT A MAGIC WAND?
# I WISH I WAS PRESIDENT!!
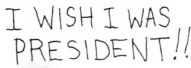

GEE, THATS ODD! IT ALWAYS WORKS FOR THEM!!

☆ SMEK
DOES IT HAVE ANYTHING TO DO WITH FOOTBALL?

CAN I FEED IT TO THE DOG?

EWWWWWW! NO!

DOES IT HAVE MONEY ROLLED UP IN IT?!

IS IT A VALUABLE ANTIQUE?!?

DOES IT HOLD THE SECRETS OF THE UNIVERSE?
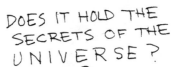
OMMMM   OMMMM
PROVE IT
SHOULD I MEDITATE WITH IT? WHAT??

HEY! WAKE UP, YOU RUDE, DEAD, LYIN' MOTHERFUCKER!! THIS IS NOT THE RIGHT ONE!! I HATE YOU ALL!!

YOU MAKE IT OUT TO BE SUCH A BIG DEAL AN' THEN I'M ALWAYS DISAPPOINTED!!

SIGH! I'LL JUST GET RID OF THIS PIECE-A SHIT AN' GO FINISH MY WALK.
RRRR

RISE N SHINE! WORK TO DO!

THE GODDESS SAID SO.

HOTHEAD SPIES ONE LUMBERING FEAR-LESSLY DOWN THE STREET

not fair!

she scares the fuck out of it...

EEEEEEEE

HUH? WHAT TH FUK!!

and quickly dispenses disability...

OOOO!

an' then...

So! LET'S REVIEW! you think women like this?

Hey babe, I know ya WANTED it! I could tell cause ya LOOKED at me!

I cant believe this is happening!

oh why me?

Im so ashamed!

I was just minding my own business..

you make my heart beat

SO, BUTTHOLE, THESE ARE THE QUALITIES THAT WOMEN WANT, RIGHT? (That's not hurting you, is it?) Ya know, YOU'RE RIGHT!

PAIN VICTIMIZATION GUILT
VIOLENCE HUMILIATION
EMOTIONAL TRAUMA SHAME
FEAR DEPRESSION
INVASION SUICIDE
DISEASE

An' we wanna THANK you guys, Im glad I could return the FAVOR!

why so quiet, chum? I know, your life is finally complete + you're overwhelmed!!

Well, TA'TA + TRA LA LA! have a sparkling evening!!

I'LL never be da same

BOO        HOO

25

BUT ALL IS SOON FORGOTTEN IN A LUXURIOUS BUBBLE BATH

A MIND IS A TERRIBLE THING TO BEND

SNARF SNYAK SNYAK HYANK HYANK

BEFORE I GO OUT I'LL JUST RELAX A FEW MINUTES WITH A COUPLE POTS OF COFFEE AND A LITTLE T.V.!

DON'T DO IT MOM!

BNOIK!

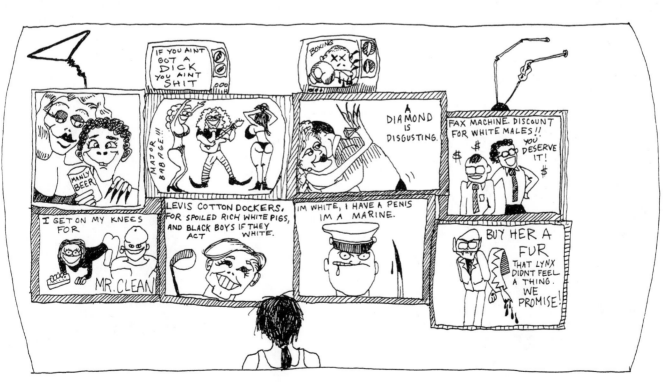

whew

CHICKEN, WHAT ARE YA THINKIN' ABOUT?

my real name

what are you thinkin' about, mom?

Joan Jett

pig

HEY, WANNA WATCH DESERT HEARTS?

AGAIN?!? oh, ok, but aren't you forgetting something??

MMBBPPLBB YYFFFBBB MBFBBD?*

PFFSSSTUMBB **

CHICKEN

* DO YOU THINK YOU CAN FIX THE PHONE?
** PROBABLY

HAVE WE HEARD OUR FAVORITE TUNE YET TODAY??

ARETHA FRANKLIN

WHATCHOO WANT
HOOT!
BABY I GOT IT
HOOT!
WHATCHOO NEED
HOOT!
WELL YA KNOW I GOT IT

ALL I'M ASKIN...

30

OH GOD HOTHEAD DON'T LEAVE ME HANGING IN MID AIR !!!!

WHEN'S THE NEXT ISSUE COMING??

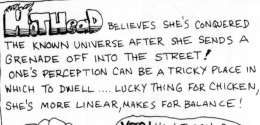

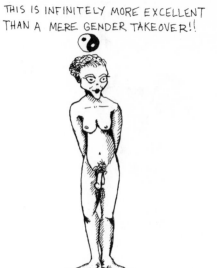

REALLY! WELL, YOU MUST'V WORKED UP QUITE AN __APPETITE__! CAN I GET YOU SOMETHING TO GNAW ON???

YOU, WHO SEEK THE ABYSS SHALL SEE THAT WHICH IS REAL.

LORD, KEEP ME SMART.

EVERYONE LOVES ME AND I'M SHRINKING.

our little bud regresses further into the haze...

THIS IS YOUR LIFE
FLASH IN THE PAN

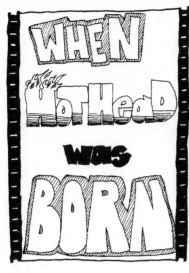

THE GODDESS SPEAKS TO OUR HEROINE IN THE WOMB...

"HOTHEAD! LITTLE HOTHEAD! WAKE UP! IT'S TIME TO BE BORN!!"

NO! I DON'T YIKE IT OUT THERE!!

"WOULD YOU PREFER TO BE STILLBORN?" THE GODDESS ASKED.

NO! THAT'S NOT MY KARMA THIS TIME! THANKS ANYWAY.

"IF IT'S SO PAINFUL FOR YOU HERE WHY DON'T YOU TAKE A BREAK FOR A MILLIENNIA OR TWO AND REMAIN IN YOUR STAR-FORM?"

ARE YOU IMPLYING THERE'S THAT MUCH TIME LEFT?? CALL ME A MASOCHIST, BUT I JUST CAN'T REST UNTIL SOME KIND OF BALANCE IS REACHED!!

"QUITE AN UNDERTAKING FOR ONE LITTLE SOUL, DON'T YOU THINK?"

I'll just do my share, I promise.

See you at intermission!

"REMEMBER HOTHEAD; WE REAP WHAT WE SOW!!!"

MY SENTIMENTS EXACTLY!!!

DOCTOR, WHY DID YOU CHOOSE OBSTETRICS?

SINCE THE "LADIES" ARE THE ONES STUCK WITH PREGNANCY, I FEEL MEN SHOULD PLAY SOME PART IN CHILDBIRTH FOR CONTROL... I MEAN SUPPORT.

DO I UNDER-STAND YOU TO BE SAYING YOU MAY FEEL A BIT INFERIOR BECAUSE YOU CAN'T REPRODUCE??

SILLY GIRLIE NURSE!! OF COURSE NOT!!! HOW IMPORTANT IS IT, ANYWAY?? IT'S JUST ONE TINY THING I CAN'T DO. SO WHAT!!

YOU ACT AS IF IT WERE A PRIVILEGE, IT'S A CURSE! YOU BITCHES DESERV... AH... OF COURSE I DON'T FEEL INFERIOR! HOW DARE YOU?!

my instincts have always told me to go to ONLY women ♀ GYNOCOLOGISTS! no wonder!

The Birth was a vacuum of calm.

COULD THAT POSSIBLY BE THE ROOT OF ALL PATRIARCHAL TYRANNY YOU PIG??? HAHHH!???

PUT A LID ON IT NURSIE!! I'VE GOT A BABY TO BIRTH!!

EEECCCHHH!!

LOOK!! I'M THE GIVER OF LIFE!! I'M THE ALPHA AND THE OMEGA!! ME!

DREAM ON FUCKFACE!

DON'T EVEN THINK OF SLAPPING ME!!

SHLIK

FVVVVVT! POOFK!

MALFUNCTION IN THE PROJECTION ROOM...

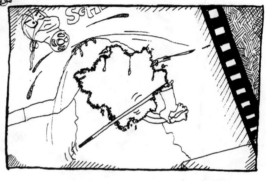

IT'S MY LITTLE PAL HOT HEAD!! OUT IN FLIP CITY AGAIN! C'MON GIRL, PULL IT IN!!

POKE POKE

OK PUPPY, GO SLOW NOW. BREATHE!! JUS' TAKE IT REAL SLOW! LET'S FIND OUR CENTER! ATTA GIRL.

GASP HASP HAR CHOKE SPLUT

I THINK I'M GETTIN' THE BENDS!!!

OH NO YOU'RE NOT! DON'T WORRY, I'M HERE. COME BACK TO EARTH.

I DON'T YIKE IT!!

YOU ARE BY FAR THE MOST DIABOLICAL WIMP I'VE EVER KNOWN!!

*ESPECIALLY INSPIRIED GENIUS ADVERTISING PLOY! USING A CAMEL AS A SEX OBJECT! NOTHING TURNS ME ON MORE THAN CAMEL-DICK! HOW DID THEY KNOW???

BUT ALAS! OUR HERO HAS NO
DISCERNIBLE ATTENTION SPAN
AND IS QUICKLY DISTRACTED...

BUT OF COURSE IT WAS AN <u>ACCIDENT</u>. WHO WOULD
HAVE THE NERVE <u>OR</u> BAD TASTE TO PULL A
STUNT LIKE THIS?!?!?

SHE FELT <u>SOOOO</u> BAD!

IS NO ONE SAFE???

SNIF! SNIF! IT SURE SMELLS
MISCHIEVOUS OUT HERE!
EVERYTHING OK, HOTHEAD?

YEAH!

SURE, SURE. COME ON NOW,
LET'S GO HOME.

MEANWHILE, BACK AT THE RATHOLE...

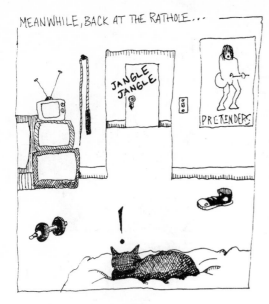

JANGLE JANGLE

PRETENDERS

!

CHICKEN!!

MOM!

OH MOMS CHICKEN BABY!! I MISSED MY BABY CHICKEN! OH MOMS L'IL TURKEY CAT!!

I LOVE MY CAT CAT CAT!!!

A REDEEMING QUALITY!

FTW

OH PURR!

SO GET IN ALREADY!! YOU SMELL LIKE AN APE!!

YI!

SO... HAVE YOU EVER THOUGHT ABOUT GOING TO THERAPY?

AHHHHH!

YOU COULD GET A LOT OF RELIEF, YOU KNOW, MAYBE IT'S ABOUT TIME YOU STARTED THINKIN' ABOUT GROWIN' UP...

40

I MEAN, I CAN'T HELP BUT THINKING THAT SOMEONE WITH YOUR ENERGY COULD MOVE MOUNTAINS IF THEY WANTED TO.

AN' BEIN SO PISSED OFF ALL THE TIME IS EVEN WORSE FOR YOU THAN RED MEAT!!

SOUP'S ON!!

NO! NO! NO! NO! NO!

I JUST **LOVE** WHEN YOU COME TO VISIT, ROZ.

OL' BUDDY, OL' PAL, OL' BUDDY OL' PAL

PURRRRR PURRRRR

THIS DOESN'T LOOK SO BAD!!

ONIONS, LETTUCE, TOMATO, MUSHROOMS, CHEESE, SOY SAUCE, AND WHAT'S THIS? ORGANIC PUBIC HAIR?

THOSE ARE SPROUTS! SPROUTS!!

HEY ROZ, YOU DON'T THINK I'M ANY LESS OF A DYKE BECAUSE OF WHAT I EAT, DO YOU??

NOT UNLESS IT'S **DICK!!** HYUK HYUK HYUK!!!

KAK.

CHICKEN

YOU ARE JUST A COMEDIC FESTIVAL TODAY!! LISTEN, SOME RIGID DYKE WITH A POLE UP HER ASS ONCE TOLD ME I WASN'T A RADICAL LESBIAN **IN HER BOOK** CAUSE I EAT MEAT AND TALK ABOUT SEX OUT LOUD!!

SHE WAS TRYIN' TO LAY ALL THE CONDITIONS ON ME, AND THEN SHE'S OUT THERE PROTESTING + LOBBYING FOR RIGHTS AN' ACCEPTANCE! WHAT A FUCKIN' **HYPOCRITE!!**

AN' I NEVER SAID I WAS A RADICAL LESBIAN!! I DON'T UNDERSTAND THAT TERM! WOULDN'T A **TRULY** RADICAL LESBIAN SLEEP WITH MEN?? WOULDN'T THAT BE THE MOST RADICAL THING A LESBIAN COULD DO?? IS IT RADICAL **COMMA** LESBIAN OR WHAT??

SO! YOU CAN'T STAND OTHER LESBIANS' INTOLERANCE OF YOU! COULD THIS POSSIBLY BE THE SAME INTOLERANCE THAT YOU HAVE TOWARD MEN? THEY'RE JUST VICTIMS OF SOCIALIZATION TOO, YOU KNOW.

**THAT'S DIFFERENT!!**

THEY ARE **NOT** VICTIMS!! THEY'RE **PREDATORS!!** THEY **HATE** ME!! I HAVE TO BE ON GUARD!!

BUT IF EVERYONE WOULD JUST DO UNTO OTHERS...

HAH! LET ME KNOW WHEN **THAT** HAPPENS AN' I'LL JOIN RIGHT IN!!

OH, SO YOU WON'T TILL THEY DO TILL YOU DO TILL THEY DO TILL...

DO ME A FAVOR FOR A SECOND? IMAGINE IF EVERYONE JUST STOPPED ALL THEIR BULLSHIT AT THE SAME TIME!!

THAT'S SIMPLISTIC! IT'S IDEALISTIC WHY, THAT WOULD BE...

pretty fucking cool.

BUT IT'LL NEVER HAPPEN!!

NOT WITH THAT ATTITUDE IT WON'T. DON'T ENCOURAGE HER, CHICKEN

CAN'T HELP IT

BUT ROZ! EVERYWHERE YA GO IT'S MONGO PHOBIA!!

YUP

I GET AS MUCH SHIT FROM THE POLITICALLY CORRECT POLICE AS I DO FROM ANYBODY ELSE!!

SHE'S GOT GEL IN HER HAIR.

TSK! TSK!

SAVE 'EM

WHAT COULD BE WORSE THAN BEING IN TH'CLOSET AROUND GAY PEOPLE???

NOT MUCH!

I MEAN, LIKE, I HATE THOSE STUPID THINGS YOU WEAR ON YOUR FEET...

AND I HATE YOUR STUPID OH·SO·COOL DOC MARTENS...

But of course everyone loves WHITE BOOTS!

BUT I WOULD NEVER NOT BE YOUR FRIEND BECAUSE OF IT!!!

SOME OF MY BEST FRIENDS ARE PUNKS.

OKAY, OH MIGHTY HEAD OF HOTNESS, IT'S BEEN A LONG DAY. PLEASE SIT DOWN AN' RELAX AND I'LL BRING YOU SOME TEA. DOES THAT SOUND GOOD TO YOUR INNER BRAT?

GOO GOO FUCKIN' GA GA

HI!

HI! DID YOU EAT?

C'MERE LEMME SMELL THE CAT BREATH!! SCHNURRRFFFF AHHHHH! SHRIMP DINNER OH CHICKEN! SNIVVVVVL

'Scuse me Hothead, But if I have to draw that fucking bathrobe one more time I'm gonna lose it. Would you please put this T-shirt on?

WHAT IF I DON'T **WANT** TO?

IT WAS JUST A QUESTION!

don't forget where you came from, honey.

?

SHIT! I DIDN'T ORDER ANY HUMBLE PIE!

**OW** CHICKEN, EASY!!

KNEAD KNEAD

WHY DON'T YOU READ TO ME OUT OF THE NEW ISSUE OF "QUEER BRAINS" MAGAZINE?

SCUM MANIFESTO V. SOLANAS

INFORM ME OF ANY IMPORTANT POLITICAL ADVANCES FOR GAYS!

OH, DIDN'T YOU HEAR? THERES A **RUMOR** THAT THEY JUST PASSED THE HOUSE IN <u>NORTH DAKOTA</u> WITH A BILL MAKING IT LEGAL FOR US TO **TAKE A SHIT !!** ANY DAY NOW WE'LL BE ROLLING IN DOOKIE TO OUR HEART'S CONTENT !!!

OH LET'S SEE NOW! WHAT OTHER GEMS ARE THERE? HOW 'BOUT **HOT GUYS IN UNIFORMS...**

ARE WAITING FOR YOUR CALL!

CALL **333-HARD!** WAIT! WANT TO ORDER A **HI-TECH ENLARGER?** HOW 'BOUT A VIDEO OF A SKINNY CROSS-EYED 17 YEAR OLD BOY??

I KNOW!! SOME **INSTANT BUTT** UNDERWEAR!!

**ANAL PROBES** IN AN ASSORTMENT OF SIZES!! **UNCUT MEN** VIDEO!! HERE'S AN **AIDS** AD WITH TWO WHITE GUYS!! ORDER A QUEER BRAINS **MUG!** THE GAY MEN'S BED + BREAKFAST GUIDE!! AN' DON'T FORGET THE **PERSONALS!!!**

WHO CARES IF HE HAS TWO HEADS... HE'S GOT 10 INCHES!!

1·900·TWO·PUDS

WHAT IS IT?

KING DONG

44

45

SIMON-PURE BIEDERMEIR!!

WHAT ARE YOU DOING IN THERE??

THIS COMIC IS TOO VIOLENT!

OH YEAH?? WHAT ABOUT BAT-FUCK AND NINTENDO AND THE ROAD RUNNER??

THAT'S DIFFERENT!! BOYS WILL BE BOYS,* YOU KNOW!!

HISSSSS

OH, GO KILL YERSELF!

* BUT GIRLS WILL BE WOMEN!! (ANONYMOUS)

SCHK! SCK SCHK SCHK SCHK SCHK SCHK SCHK SCHK SCHK

FTT FTT FTT FTT FTT FTT FTT FTT

ALRIGHT CHICKEN!!

SLAM

HAIL CHICKEN!! FEARLESS DEFENDER OF CIVIL RIGHTS!!

THE LONG ARM OF THE PAW!

WHEW ROZ, I THINK IM DEFINITELY OUT OF GAS THIS TIME.

YUP. I THINK IT'S ABOUT TIME I GROPED MY WAY HOME.

PURRRR PURRRR

WHAT IS THIS STUFF ANYWAY? VALIUM TEA?

YOU'RE A TRUE 20TH CENTURY CASUALTY. IT'S CHAMOMILE.

49

58

INDEED, ALL OVER TOWN...

NOBODY KNOWS I'M A LESBIAN

YA BETTER GO NOW!

HET SPRAY

PUT ONE ON BEFORE YOU PUT IT IN

COFFEE JIG EVERYDAY 4 P.M. at THE DICK KNOT

PSSSSST! YA WANNA SEE SOMETHIN' REALLY DISGUSTING?

ORT!

CINEMA

ART FART CINEMA

CINEMA I
THELMA + LOUISE

CINEMA II
THE SALTING OF THE HAMS
WITH: THE REIL BEEF-CAKE

WOMENCRAFTS
BOOKS · JEWELRY · MUSIC

OPEN

5% LESBO DISCOUNT

376

HETS-B-GONE

QUEERS ARE SUCH ANGELS!

CHICKEN, STOP VOGUEING!

I DON'T DO BOYS

SPIRITUS

CAPPUCCINO SHAKE

I'M IN LOVE WITH THIS PLACE! SUN, WAVES, DANCIN', CLAMS an' GAY-OWNED EVERYTHING!

WHAT IS IT WITH QUEERS AND THE OCEAN, ANYWAY? P-TOWN, OGUNQUIT, SAN FRAN, KEY WEST....

AN' DON'T FORGET SHOP·A·RAMA!

P-TOWN

**HotHead** IS ABOUT TO commune WITH ALL THAT IS in the dream state. Oh boy Oh boy.

(BEWARE OF PEOPLE WHO SLEEP FLAT ON THEIR BACK.)

THEY DON'T USE PHYSICAL BODIES HERE BUT I'LL PUT THEM ANYWAY OR ELSE THE NEXT FEW PANELS WILL BE REALLY BORING.

NOT LIKE THE I-MADE-OUT-WITH-DEBBIE-HARRY-DREAM STATE, OR EVEN THE MY-UNCLE-VITO-WHO'S-BEEN-DEAD-FOR 20-YEARS-APPEARED-AS-A-RAT-AND-TOLD-ME-TO-LOOK-IN-THE WASHING MACHINE DREAM STATE...

EGO CHECK

HOTHEAD APPROACHES THE ONE WHO HAS ALL THE ANSWERS.. AND YA KNOW SHE HAS QUESTIONS‼

BUT A REALLY, REALLY DEEP PLACE, AND THOSE WHO DWELL THERE KNOW THAT YOU'RE THE DREAM!

PLUTO PROBLEMS? 1-800-TRANSIT

THE TRICK IS TO BRING THE INFORMATION BACK TO THE CONSCIOUS LEVEL.

HULLO? IS THERE AN INFINITE WISDOM IN THE HOUSE?

can't see a @*!!!# thing!

ONLY A VERY AWARE, SPIRITUAL, INWARDLY TUNED AND HIGHLY PSYCHIC TYPE CAN DO IT!

SO WE KNOW HOTHEAD DOESN'T HAVE A CHANCE.

BUT OF COURSE HER GUARDIAN ANGEL WILL FILE IT FOR HER.

OHM

ALRIGHT CUT THE CRAP! WHERE ARE YA???

HOTHEAD PAISAN © 1991 DIANE DIMASSA

62

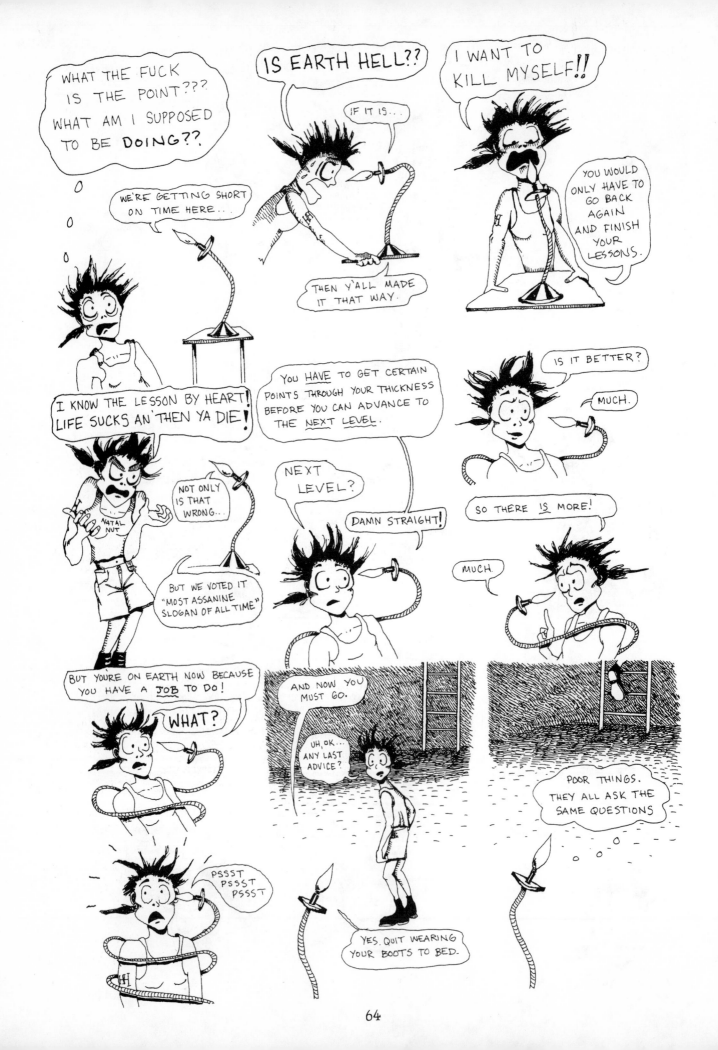

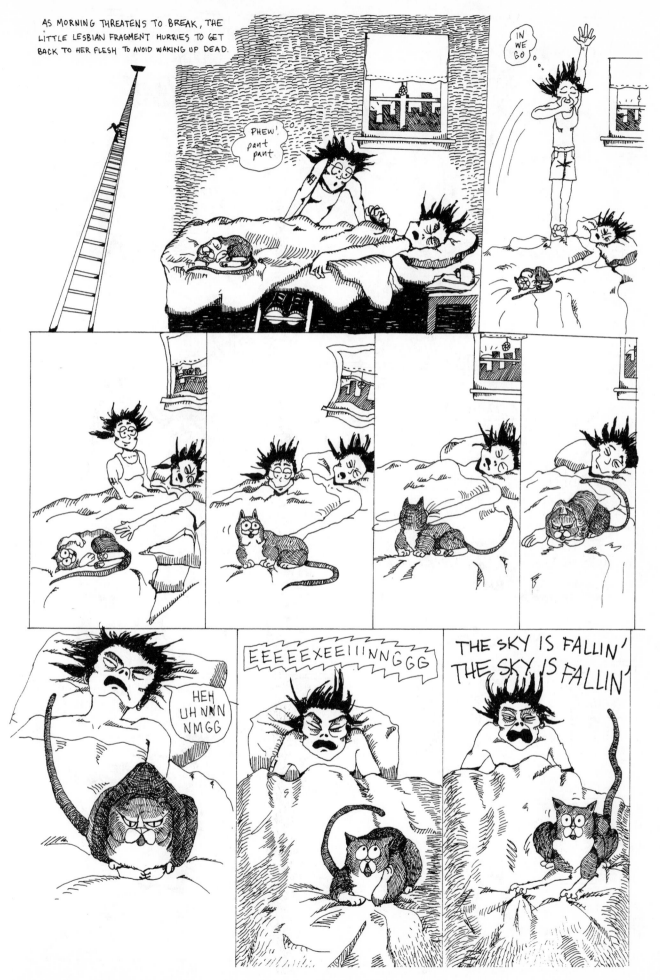

65

66

74

76

IS YOUR CAREER SUFFERING DUE TO UNWORTHY PENISES??

ARE YOU TIRED OF FEARING FOR YOUR LIFE BECAUSE PENISES ARE STALKING THE PLANET?

HAVE YOU EVER BEEN TERRORIZED BY AN UNWANTED PENIS?

WOULD YOU LIKE TO IMPROVE THE QUALITY OF YOUR LIFE THROUGH THE TOTAL ELIMINATION OF PENISES??

THEN I AM THE GIRL 4U

CALL 1-800 BLOW-U-AWAY

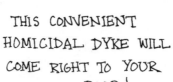

NEVER AGAIN WALK AWAY QUIETLY BECAUSE THERE'S "NOTHING U CAN DO"

THIS CONVENIENT HOMICIDAL DYKE WILL COME RIGHT TO YOUR DOOR!

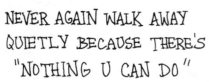

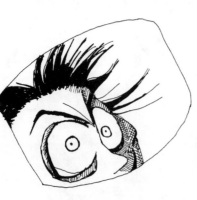

HELLO!

SO CALL NOW!
1-800-BLOW-U-AWAY
1-800-BLOW-U-AWAY
* SPECIAL SERVICES FOR INCEST + RAPE SURVIVORS *
THATS 1-800-BLOW-U-AWAY
1-800-BLOW-U-AWAY

MY NAME IS FRAN, AND I'D LIKE TO MAKE A COMMENT ON YOUR SENSIBILITY!

WHY SHORE, FRAN! JUST ONE THING, THO...

YOU CAN PUT THE PHONE DOWN. I'M RIGHT HERE.

HAH?

OK. I FIND HOTHEAD DISGUSTINGLY VIOLENT! SHE ACTS JUST LIKE THE MEN SHE'S BASHING!

WE, AS WOMEN, MUST SET AN EXAMPLE AND ACT IN A PEACE-FUL, NON-VIOLENT WAY GODAMMIT!

HOTHEAD DOESN'T KNOW THAT! SHE'S BLITZED OUT ON TOO MUCH T.V.! THE WHOLE THING IS A SATIRE ON HOW MANIPULATIVE THE MEDIA IS! DIDN'T YOU READ ISSUE #1, FRAN?

WELL, I DON'T LIKE SEEING MALE GENITALS AND BLOOD AND GORE!!

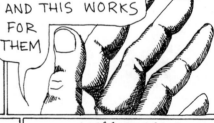

I KNOW, BUT A LOT OF WOMEN NEED TO VENT THEIR RAGE AND THIS WORKS FOR THEM

THERE ARE CONSTRUCTIVE WAYS TO VENT ANGER... LIKE PROTESTING, AND LETTER-WRITING!

LOOK! WE'RE DEALING WITH FANTASY HERE! HAVEN'T YOU EVER BEEN SO PISSED-OFF AT SOMEONE THAT YOU FANTASIZED ABOUT KILLING THEM?

LIKE MAYBE POSSIBLY YOUR UNCLE GEORGE??

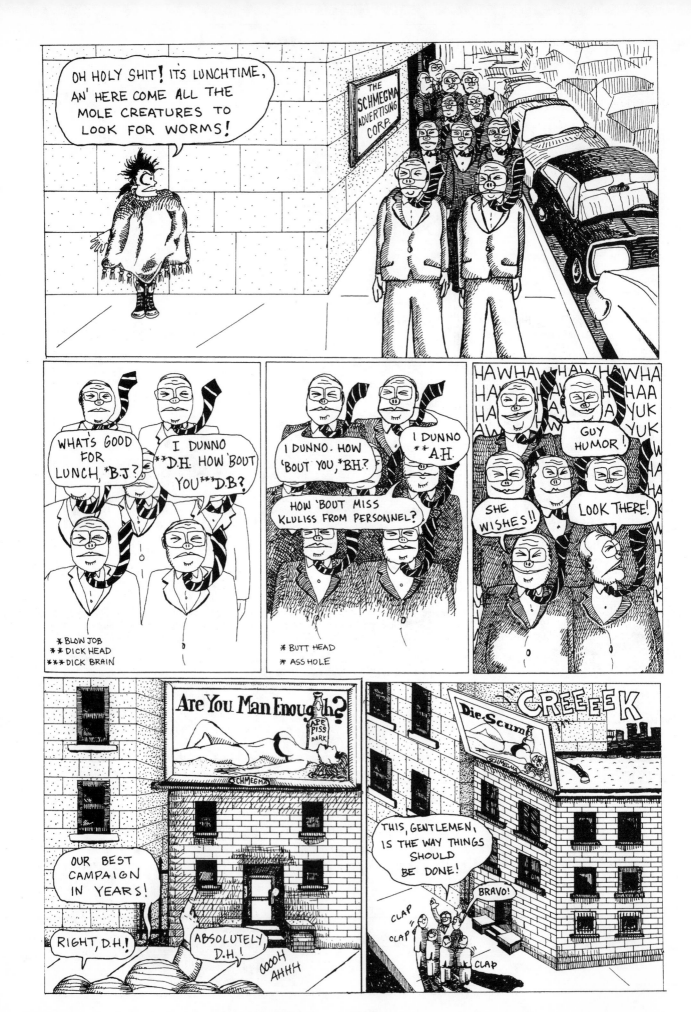

88

90

92

93

94

I'VE BEGUN A PROFILE BASED ON WHAT I KNOW SO FAR: SPASMODIC ENTHUSIASM SENSE OF INFALLIBILITY, BRUSQUE, TORTUROUS MIND, NEUROTIC, DESTRUCTIVE...

UNBRIDLED FREE EXPRESSION, PERVERSE SELF-WILL, HELL-BENT...

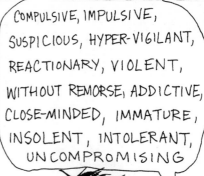

COMPULSIVE, IMPULSIVE, SUSPICIOUS, HYPER-VIGILANT, REACTIONARY, VIOLENT, WITHOUT REMORSE, ADDICTIVE, CLOSE-MINDED, IMMATURE, INSOLENT, INTOLERANT, UNCOMPROMISING

IN OTHER WORDS, LUCID!

LUCID.

CLEAR AS A BELL! QUICK AS A WHIP! TIGHT AS A DRUM!

SO, AH, IS IT SAFE TO ASSUME THAT YOU SEE NO NEED FOR CHANGE?

CHANGE?

OW!

BONK

CHANGE WHAT?

M-MAYBE TO BECOME LESS EH... TURBULENT? P-P-PERHAPS BECOME MORE CHANNELLED?

97

MEANWHILE, DOWN THE BLOCK...

THERE AINT BUT ONE PERSON WALKS LIKE THAT!!

HOTHEAD!

CHICKEN!

MERCY!

MERCY!

MAN, I WAS JUST THINKIN' ABOUT YOU! I DIDN'T KNOW YOU WERE BACK IN TOWN! BLAH BLAB BLAB AND AGITATED CHATTER BLAH BLAH BLAH

ARE YOU GOIN' TO P'TOWN? OH, P-TOWN! 'MEMBER THAT? HAHAHAHAWHAW

AHEM!

YO, WHAT??

YER BEIN' RUDE!

LEARN SOME MOTHER-FUCKIN' PATIENCE!!!

WHO YOU TELLIN?

IM TELLIN' YOU! DON'T PLAY NO FUCKIN' "AHEM" SHIT WITH ME!

I AIN'T PLAYIN' FUCKIN' NUTHIN' WITCHOO!!

I'LL CHILL YOUR MOTHERFUCKIN' ASS RIGHT OUT!!

OK, HERE GOES ALIEN MESSAGE ON ITS DOOMED MISSION TO PENETRATE THE PENILE BRAIN!

THE INFORMATION SIMPLY CANNOT BE ACCEPTED! IT HAS NOWHERE TO GO!

THIS RESULTS IN MOMENTARY UTTER CONFUSION!

↳(YOU'VE SEEN THE LOOK)

...UNTIL...

THE MESSAGE IS SUMMONED TO THE BLANKET RESPONSE OFFICE!

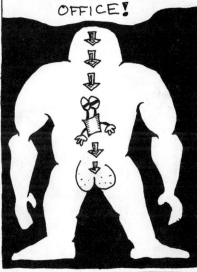

THE SUBJECT IS IMMEDIATELY MORE COMFORTABLE!

THE DISORIENTATION DISAPPEARS AND TESTOSTERONE TAKES THE PLACE OF ANY THOUGHT PROCESS!

ELAPSED TIME 00.005 secs.

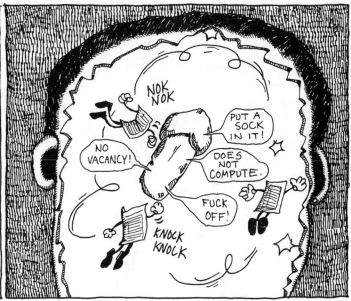

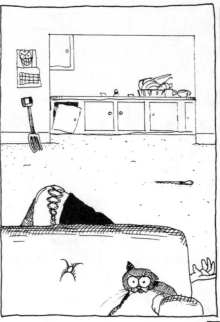

117

118

122

125

128

HOLY SHIT, LOOKIT THIS!!! "FEMININE EXTERNAL WASH" I GUESS THEY USE THIS DURING THE FEMININE STEAM CLEANING, WHERE THEY PULVERIZE THAT DISGUSTING FEMININE SMELL!!

SPEAK FOR YOURSELF

AND SO WHERE'S THE CLIT POLISH? APPLY ONLY WITH THE DISPOSABLE FEMININE BUFFING RAG!

THIGH TRIMMER
GIT IT GALS
THI TR
WOO-WOO
HEY

THE UNWANTED HAIR LINE!! GIRLS, DON'T BE CAUGHT DEAD WITH THAT BEARD HANGING OUT OF YOUR BIKINI!!

BURN IT!
TEAR IT OUT!

APPLY IT WITH THESE LOVELY SYNTHETIC COSMETIC PUFFS!!

SPACE-WEEDS
$12.99
SHELF-LIFE: TIL THE END + BEYO

OR BLEACH THAT MUSTACCHIO TO A NATURAL-LOOKING URINE-YELLOW!! THAT SIZZLING, FRYING SOUND TELLS YOU IT'S WORKING!!!

AND MY FAVE, WAXING! IT LASTS OH, SO MUCH LONGER!!

HAIR CAN'T GROW WHERE THERE'S NO SKIN!

RIP

WHY, IF I DON'T LOOK GOOD, I DON'T FEEL GOOD! WHAT'S THAT!??

MUST BE A TORTURE DEVICE!!!

YEAH! FOR PULLING OUT TONGUES!

AND LET'S MAKE SURE OUR EYEBROWS ARE JUST RIGHT!!

MY ANTENNA'S ARE PERFECT

HAVE A CUP OF **TEA** AT THE END OF A HARD DAY OF BEING BELITTLED, HUMILIATED, BERATED?

HELD DOWN, SHOVED ASIDE MOWED OVER, SWEPT UNDER

STIFLED, STUNTED, STEPPED ON, SNOWED...

HAWKED, STALKED, SMASHED, BASHED, (AND EVEN...

SIT ON MY FACE

**KILLED**

HERE LIES SOME QUEER, IT DON'T MATTER WHO. CAUSE WE DON'T CARE, AND WE'LL GET YOU, TOO!

IN CASE YA HAVEN'T NOTICED, THE WORLD AIN'T EXACTLY ON MY SIDE!

IF I DON'T DO IT, WHO WILL??

WHAT ROZ SEES →

DO WHAT?? **WHAT** ARE YOU DOING?? AND WHY ARE **YOU** THE CENTER OF THE UNIVERSE??? HOW DO YOU SUPPOSE MERCY MUST FEEL???

138

139

HAH HAH HAH

THE POWER OF THE UNIVERSE IN MY LITTLE FINGER!!!

HEY HOTHEAD! TAKE ME WITH YOU!

YOU'RE ALL COMIN'

?

HEY PEACH HEAD! SHARQUEE HERE??

YEAH, YEAH, BACK ROOM

HEY, ROCKY

mm-hmm. G'head. no trouble.

NOPE.

WELL FUCK ME! IT'S the END already!? What does Hothead think she's going to find out and WHY DOESN'T she go OUT MORE OFTEN? SEE U NEXT TIME! ♥ I LOVE YOU! ♥

143

HOTHEAD PAISAN ©1993 DIANE DiMASSA

PSSSST!

IT'S A NEW YEAR!

IN A DECADE FULL OF CHANGES, I MIGHT ADD!

THE PREZ IS A ♀

THE EARTH IS PURGING HERSELF!! ALL CONFLICTS ARE BEING BROUGHT TO THE SURFACE FOR RECONCILIATION! YUPPIES ARE GOING BANKRUPT!!

FEAR NOT

EVEN YOU'VE BEEN EXPERIENCING MILI-SECONDS OF TOLERANCE!

AND THIS NEW PRESIDENT! YOU HAVE TO ADMIT, HE'S DIFFERENT! AND HOW ABOUT HER?!?

HE'S STILL A WHITE GUY!!!

BUT THAT COULD BE THE ACE IN THE HOLE!! WHO ELSE WOULD BRAIN-DEAD MIDDLE AMERICA LISTEN TO?? AND ALL THE WHILE, HE'S ADVOCATING A BELIEF SYSTEM THAT'S A LOT LIKE YOURS!!

WHY DONTCHA QUIT BEING SUCH A HATEFUL ON-SIGHT BIGOT! THERE'S MORE AND MORE PEOPLE EVERY DAY CHANGING THEIR EVIL WAYS - AND SOME OF THEM ARE MEN - WHITE ONES, EVEN!!

Idgie

145

146

150

151

LISTEN, I KNOW MOST MEN SUCK, BUT THEY'RE NOT ALL POISONED! I KNOW SOME NICE ONES!

WHY'D JA TAKE YOUR ARM AWAY?

HMPH

CROSS NOW AND DIE

DAN QUAYLE MEMORIAL GARBAGE CAN

THE GUYS I GO OUT WITH ARE MORE LIKE WOMEN, REALLY! YOU'D PROBABLY LIKE THEM! AND ANYWAY, YOU'RE RIPPING YOURSELF OFF BY CUTTING A WHOLE GENDER OUT OF YOUR EXPERIENCE!

SUZETTE, YOU KNOW I LOVE YOU, BUT THERE'S A BIG PART OF YOU I JUST CAN'T RELATE TO!

1-800-PRINCESS-PIZZA

PHONE

MY ONLY INTEREST IN MEN IS SQUASHING THEM BEFORE THEY SQUASH ME!!. I FEEL NO COMPASSION, AND DEFINITELY NO ATTRACTION! I JUST DON'T UNDERSTAND YOU!!

I'M SICK OF HAVING THIS SAME ARGUMENT EVERY TIME I SEE YOU! DON'T TAKE YOUR BELIEF SYSTEM OUT ON ME!!!

WELL THEN QUIT ASKIN' ME WHEN WE'RE GETTIN' MARRIED!! YOU KNOW WHAT I'M GONNA SAY!! JUST DON'T BRING IT UP!!

YOU'RE SO... SO...

HEY BAYBEE!

154

157

158

159

163

LOOK, I LOVE YOU NO MATTER WHAT YOU DO!

I KNOW. IT'S SO WEIRD.

JUST GO FINISH LIVING YOUR LIFE AND DO THE BEST YOU CAN. BUT PAY MORE ATTENTION TO THESE PEOPLE!!

NOW I'D LIKE TO GIVE YOU A LITTLE DOSE OF...

OF WHAT?

LOVE, BABY! I'M GOING TO GIVE YOU A TEENY, TINY IDEA OF WHAT REAL LOVE FEELS LIKE!

PHOOEY!

HERE WE GO! WE'LL START YOU OFF NICE AND LIGHT! WOULDN'T WANT YOUR LITTLE HUMAN BODY TO EXPLODE!

THIS IS JUST SO IT GETS IN YOUR MEMORY BANK NOT TO MESS WITH THE ULTIMATE FORCE!

HEE HEE HEE! THEY'RE JUST NOT BUILT TO RESIST!

168

170

# About the Author

**D**IANE DIMASSA is a ferocious cartoonist of 30+ years residing on the East Coast. She has been cartooning and drawing since she was a little child, stopping only to take drugs for 15 years. After extensive field work, she was awarded an honorary degree in self-destruction and went on to the University of Rehab, where she graduated with honors. She has been prolific ever since. Her work is message-oriented and serves to heal.

# LETTERS FROM OUR FANS

"This could scare Patty Hearst..." —*Ann, Waterbury, CT*

"My local Queers R Us doesn't have the new issue yet so...I stabbed them in the head 25 times..." —*Jody, Ocala, FL*

"Yet another convert to action. Having just escaped the Bible Belt of central California, I greatly appreciate your outstanding drawing and prose—HH is fearless. Sign me up!" —*Amy, Athens, GA*

"I am a total Hothead junkie and just wanted to tell you how fucking cool you are..." —*Amy, Northampton, MA*

"I think you should marry me. My girlfriend, Heather, says she'll let you marry me if you promise to lick her feet and call her Ma'am." —*Joyce, Gainesville, FL*

"You are dangerous." —*Kate, P'Town, MA*

"...from the first moment I laid eyes on HH, it was love. I think she's my dream woman, and she should DEFINITELY NOT GET THERAPY." —*Anonymous, New York, NY*

"Alright, how long have you been following me around and reading my mind!?!?" —*Lee Lightning, Seattle, WA*

"I'm thoroughly enamored of Chicken." —*Lee, OR*

"I have a question: you mentioned some fag cartoonist who never draws dykes. Who is it?" —*Robert Kirby, Minneapolis, MN*

"You are a truly disturbed individual." —*Straight White Chick, Bible Belt, TN*

"I am trying to figure out this stupid world. This bitch needs a subscription." —*Kate, Swannanoa, NC*

"I can be just as pissed in a dress, I really can!" —*Michaela, San Francisco, CA*

"The Lesbian Nations thank you...Trouble is we can hardly ever find the current issue when we want it. Dykes drag it all over the place. I've found it in the darkroom, under the kitchen table, and a couple of weeks ago, I actually found it on the back of the second floor toilet. No shit." —*Polly, Thistlethwaite, Lesbian Herstory Archive, New York*

"Please convey my undying love and devotion to Chicken." —*Cheryl, Newark, NJ*

"So what exactly is Chicken's gender? I'm asking on behalf of my Tabby Pie." —*S., Greely, CO*

"Chicken is a most agreeable name for anything." —*J., Evanston, IL*

"Please say Chicken is committed. Otherwise my wife may leave me to go after her." —*Drama, Santa Cruz, CA*

"Why is it that your drawings of Chicken's feet do me in!??!" —*Lee, Seattle, WA*

"Dangle your butt lint before me like pearls before swine." —*Joyce, Gainesville, FL*

"I have my period so I don't have to study tonight, HAHAHAHAHA!" —*Hopey, Albany, NY*

"I'd love to go over to the White House without a tampon and bleed all over the G-damn lawn. I think I will." —*Sue, Washington, DC*

"Finding your comic was like finding an island in the middle of a sea of turpentine." —*Erin, Hyattsville, MD*

"Here I've been in an evil mood all day, and now, looking at this little cartoon book, I'm giggling and laughing. So what kind of drug do you smear the paper with?" —*Lee, Seattle, WA*

"You are the last hope in a country where 'PC-ness' means 'let's not bash the poor white males who just can't help themselves.'" —*Jennifer, Lewisdale, MD*

"My household has been known to spontaneously break into Hothead dialogue." —*Miriam, Northampton, MA*

"Damn, if Hothead had breasts like Susan Sarandon, she'd be perfect." —*Liz O'Lexa, Minneapolis, MN*

"I love the little Paisan more than anything in the whole wide world, excerpt maybe a nice orange kitty or k.d. lang in a black leather jacket." —*Lesley, San Francisco, CA*

"Maybe what Hothead needs is a cute, bald sexworker who likes to wear little dresses with her doc martens." —*Jessica, San Francisco, CA*

"I would pray to you except you're still alive." —*T., Philadelphia, PA*

"I was baking my head in the oven when the newest issue came in the mail..." —*Ann, New London, CT*

"Tis better to be homicidal than suicidal." —*Sue, Fort Pierce, FL*

"Personally speaking, it's been a slow year for terrorism, except of course the giant inflatable BUD MAN whose throat I cut." —*Sarah, Madison, NJ*

"I yearn uncontrollably for those cutoff pajama shorts." —*Nytsirk, Montreal*

"I wish I was a cartoonist so I could draw the knuckle draggers that come into the convenience store where I work." —*Mary, Salley, SC*

"I walk real loud and tall now and I don't waver." —*Connie, Madison, WI*

"Keep up the pig killing! Damn! It feels good!" —*Carolyn, Topanga, CA*

"'Oh Purr' yourselves!" —*Mimi, Oakland, CA*

"Hothead: the thinking woman's alter ego." —*Kathleen, Elgin, IL*

"Stress formula: Hothead and ten minutes primal scream and pillow kicking daily." —*Eva, Bryn Mawr, PA*

"We can do this, yeah, we *are* doing this." —*Yvette Rage, Brooklyn, NY*

"Peace on earth. Farewell to men." —*Anonymous*

# BOOKS FROM CLEIS PRESS

## CARTOONS

**Hothead Paisan: Homicidal Lesbian Terrorist**
by Diane DiMassa.
ISBN: 0-939416-73-5 $12.95 paper.

**The Night Audrey's Vibrator Spoke: A Stonewall Riots Collection**
by Andrea Natalie.
ISBN: 0-939416-64-6 $8.95 paper.

**Rubyfruit Mountain: A Stonewall Riots Collection**
by Andrea Natalie.
ISBN: 0-939416-74-3 $9.95 paper.

## LESBIAN STUDIES

**Boomer: Railroad Memoirs**
by Linda Niemann.
ISBN: 0-939416-55-7 $12.95 paper.

**The Case of the Not-So-Nice Nurse**
by Mabel Maney.
ISBN: 0-939416-75-1 $24.95 cloth;
ISBN: 0-039416-76-X $9.95 paper.

**Daughters of Darkness: Lesbian Vampire Stories**
edited by Pam Keesey.
ISBN: 0-939416-77-8 $24.95 cloth;
ISBN: 0-939416-78-6 $9.95 paper.

**Different Daughters: A Book by Mothers of Lesbians**
edited by Louise Rafkin.
ISBN: 0-939416-12-3 $21.95 cloth;
ISBN: 0-939416-13-1 $9.95 paper.

**Different Mothers: Sons & Daughters of Lesbians Talk About Their Lives**
edited by Louise Rafkin.
ISBN: 0-939416-40-9 $24.95 cloth;
ISBN: 0-939416-41-7 $9.95 paper.

**A Lesbian Love Advisor**
by Celeste West.
ISBN: 0-939416-27-1 $24.95 cloth;
ISBN: 0-939416-26-3 $9.95 paper.

**Long Way Home: The Odyssey of a Lesbian Mother and Her Children**
by Jeanne Jullion.
ISBN: 0-939416-05-0 $8.95 paper.

**More Serious Pleasure: Lesbian Erotic Stories and Poetry**
edited by the Sheba Collective.
ISBN: 0-939416-48-4 $24.95 cloth;
ISBN: 0-939416-47-6 $9.95 paper.

**Queer and Pleasant Danger: Writing Out My Life**
by Louise Rafkin.
ISBN: 0-939416-60-3 $24.95 cloth;
ISBN: 0-939416-61-1 $9.95 paper.

**Serious Pleasure: Lesbian Erotic Stories and Poetry**
edited by the Sheba Collective.
ISBN: 0-939416-46-8 $24.95 cloth;
ISBN: 0-939416-45-X $9.95 paper.

## SEXUAL POLITICS

**Good Sex: Real Stories from Real People**
by Julia Hutton.
ISBN: 0-939416-56-5 $24.95 cloth;
ISBN: 0-939416-57-3 $12.95 paper.

**Madonnarama: Essays on Sex and Popular Culture**
edited by Lisa Frank and Paul Smith.
ISBN: 0-939416-72-7 $24.95 cloth;
ISBN: 0-939416-71-9 $9.95 paper.

**Sex Work: Writings by Women in the Sex Industry**
edited by Frédérique Delacoste and Priscilla Alexander.
ISBN: 0-939416-10-7 $24.95 cloth;
ISBN: 0-939416-11-5 $16.95 paper.

**Susie Bright's Sexual Reality: A Virtual Sex World Reader**
by Susie Bright.
ISBN: 0-939416-58-1 $24.95 cloth;
ISBN: 0-939416-59-X $9.95 paper.

**Susie Sexpert's Lesbian Sex World**
by Susie Bright.
ISBN: 0-939416-34-4 $24.95 cloth;
ISBN: 0-939416-35-2 $9.95 paper.

## POLITICS OF HEALTH

**The Absence of the Dead Is Their Way of Appearing**
by Mary Winfrey Trautmann.
ISBN: 0-939416-04-2 $8.95 paper.

**AIDS: The Women**
edited by Ines Rieder and Patricia Ruppelt.
ISBN: 0-939416-20-4 $24.95 cloth;
ISBN: 0-939416-21-2 $9.95 paper

**Don't: A Woman's Word**
by Elly Danica.
ISBN: 0-939416-23-9 $21.95 cloth;
ISBN: 0-939416-22-0 $8.95 paper

**1 in 3: Women with Cancer Confront an Epidemic**
edited by Judith Brady.
ISBN: 0-939416-50-6 $24.95 cloth;
ISBN: 0-939416-49-2 $10.95 paper.

**Voices in the Night: Women Speaking About Incest**
edited by Toni A.H. McNaron and Yarrow Morgan.
ISBN: 0-939416-02-6 $9.95 paper.

**With the Power of Each Breath: A Disabled Women's Anthology**
edited by Susan Browne, Debra Connors and Nanci Stern.
ISBN: 0-939416-09-3 $24.95 cloth;
ISBN: 0-939416-06-9 $10.95 paper.

**Woman-Centered Pregnancy and Birth**
by the Federation of Feminist Women's Health Centers.
ISBN: 0-939416-03-4 $11.95 paper.

## FICTION

**Another Love**
by Erzsébet Galgóczi.
ISBN: 0-939416-52-2 $24.95 cloth;
ISBN: 0-939416-51-4 $8.95 paper.

**Cosmopolis: Urban Stories by Women**
edited by Ines Rieder.
ISBN: 0-939416-36-0 $24.95 cloth;
ISBN: 0-939416-37-9 $9.95 paper.

**A Forbidden Passion**
by Cristina Peri Rossi.
ISBN: 0-939416-64-0 $24.95 cloth;
ISBN: 0-939416-68-9 $9.95 paper.

**In the Garden of Dead Cars**
by Sybil Claiborne.
ISBN: 0-939416-65-4 $24.95 cloth;
ISBN: 0-939416-66-2 $9.95 paper.

**Night Train To Mother**
by Ronit Lentin.
ISBN: 0-939416-29-8 $24.95 cloth;
ISBN: 0-939416-28-X $9.95 paper.

**The One You Call Sister: New Women's Fiction**
edited by Paula Martinac.
ISBN: 0-939416-30-1 $24.95 cloth;
ISBN: 0-939416031-X $9.95 paper.

**Only Lawyers Dancing**
by Jan McKemmish.
ISBN: 0-939416-70-0 $24.95 cloth;
ISBN: 0-939416-69-7 $9.95 paper.

**Unholy Alliances: New Women's Fiction**
edited by Louise Rafkin.
ISBN: 0-939416-14-X $21.95 cloth;
ISBN: 0-939416-15-8 $9.95 paper.

**The Wall**
by Marlen Haushofer.
ISBN: 0-939416-53-0 $24.95 cloth;
ISBN: 0-939416-54-9 $9.95 paper.

## LATIN AMERICA

**Beyond the Border: A New Age in Latin American Women's Fiction**
edited by Nora Erro-Peralta and Caridad Silva-Núñez.
ISBN: 0-939416-42-5 $24.95 cloth;
ISBN: 0-939416-43-3 $12.95 paper.

**The Little School: Tales of Disappearance and Survival in Argentina**
by Alicia Partnoy.
ISBN: 0-939416-08-5 $21.95 cloth;
ISBN: 0-939416-07-7 $9.95 paper.

**Revenge of the Apple**
by Alicia Partnoy.
ISBN: 0-939416-62-X $24.95 cloth;
ISBN: 0-939416-63-8 $8.95 paper.

**You Can't Drown the Fire: Latin American Women Writing in Exile**
edited by Alicia Partnoy.
ISBN: 0-939416-16-6 $24.95 cloth;
ISBN: 0-939416-17-4 $9.95 paper.

## AUTOBIOGRAPHY, BIOGRAPHY, LETTERS

**Peggy Deery: An Irish Family at War**
by Nell McCafferty.
ISBN: 0-939416-38-7 $24.95 cloth;
ISBN: 0-939416-39-5 $9.95 paper.

**The Shape of Red: Insider/Outsider Reflections**
by Ruth Hubbard and Margaret Randall.
ISBN: 0-939416-19-0 $24.95 cloth;
ISBN: 0-939416-18-2 $9.95 paper.

**Women & Honor: Some Notes on Lying**
by Adrienne Rich.
ISBN: 0-939416-44-1 $3.95 paper.

## ANIMAL RIGHTS

**And a Deer's Ear, Eagle's Song and Bear's Grace: Relationships Between Animals and Women**
edited by Theresa Corrigan and Stephanie T. Hoppe.
ISBN: 0-939416-38-7 $24.95 cloth;
ISBN: 0-939416-39-5 $9.95 paper.

**With a Fly's Eye, Whale's Wit and Woman's Heart: Relationships Between Animals and Women**
edited by Theresa Corrigan and Stephanie T. Hoppe.
ISBN: 0-939416-24-7 $24.95 cloth;
ISBN: 0-939416-25-5 $9.95 paper.

## TO ORDER BOOKS

Since 1980, Cleis Press has published progressive books by women. We welcome your order and will ship your books as quickly as possible. Individual orders must be prepaid (U.S. dollars only). Please add 15% shipping. Pennsylvania residents add 6% sales tax. Mail orders to Cleis Press, P.O. Box 8933, Pittsburgh, PA 15221. MasterCard and Visa orders: include account number, expiration date, and signature. Fax your credit card order to (412) 937-1567. Or telephone us Monday through Friday, 9 am–5 pm Eastern Standard Time, at (412) 937-1555.